Common Core
Standards Practice Workbook

Grade 2

Glenview, Illinois • Boston, Massachusetts
Chandler, Arizona • Upper Saddle River, New Jersey

ALWAYS LEARNING

PEARSON

PEARSON

ISBN-13: 978-0-328-75685-8
ISBN-10:   0-328-75685-7

20 20

Grade 2 Contents

 **Standards Practice**

 **Assessment**

About this Workbook

Pearson is pleased to offer this **Common Core Standards Practice Workbook**. In it, you will find pages to help you become good math thinkers and problem-solvers. It includes these pages:

- **Common Core Standards Practice pages.** For each Common Core Standard, you will find two pages of practice exercises. On these pages, you will find different kinds of exercises that are similar to the items expected to be on the end-of-year assessments you will be taking starting in Grade 3. Some of the exercises will have more than one correct answer! Be sure to read each exercise carefully and be on the look-out for exercises that ask you to circle "all that apply" or "all that are correct." They will likely have more than one correct answer.

- **Practice for the Common Core Assessment.** You will find a practice assessment, similar to the Next Generation Assessment that you will be taking. The Practice End-of-Year Assessment has 40 items that are all aligned to the Common Core Standards for Mathematical Content. The two Performance Tasks focus on assessing the Standards for Mathematical Practice.

Name _____

Common Core Standards Practice

2.OA.A.1 Use addition and subtraction within 100 to solve one- and two-step word problems involving situations of adding to, taking from, putting together, taking apart, and comparing, with unknowns in all positions, e.g., by using drawings and equations with a symbol for the unknown number to represent the problem.

1. Samantha has 6 toy cars.

Roger has 10 toy cars.

How many do they have in all?

_____

....

2. Tim has 29 stickers.

Maya has 14 fewer stickers than Tim.

Draw a model to match the story problem.

How many stickers does Maya have?

_____

3. Emma has 53 marbles.
She gets some marbles from Fred.
Then she gives 10 marbles to Tessie.
She now has 58 marbles.
How many marbles does she get from Fred?

Write a number sentence to solve.
Use ? for the unknown.

____ ◯ ____ ◯ ____ ◯ ____

Solve the number sentence.

_____

4. Allison buys 25 roses and some tulips.
She loses 4 flowers on her way home.
At home, she counts 30 flowers.
How many tulips did she buy?

Draw a model to match the story problem.

Solve the number sentence.

_____

Name _____

Common Core Standards Practice

2.OA.B.2 Fluently add and subtract within 20 using mental strategies. By end of Grade 2, know from memory all sums of two one-digit numbers.

Solve.

1. 7 + 12 = ☐

ⓐ 20

Ⓑ 19

Ⓒ 12

Ⓓ 15

2. 8 + 9 = ☐

ⓐ 20

Ⓑ 19

Ⓒ 17

Ⓓ 15

3. 13 − 7 = ☐

_____

4. 13 + 6 = ☐

_____

5. 14 − 6 = ☐

_____

6. 19 − 5 = ☐

_____

7. $18 - 9 =$ ☐

Ⓐ 7

Ⓑ 8

Ⓒ 9

Ⓓ 10

8. $12 - 9 =$ ☐

Ⓐ 3

Ⓑ 4

Ⓒ 5

Ⓓ 6

9. $15 - 6 =$ ☐

———

10. $4 + 16 =$ ☐

———

11. $5 + 12 =$ ☐

———

12. $13 + 7 =$ ☐

———

CC 4

Name _____

Common Core Standards Practice

2.OA.C.3 Determine whether a group of objects (up to 20) has an odd or even number of members, e.g., by pairing objects or counting them by 2s; write an equation to express an even number as a sum of two equal addends.

1. Which shows an odd number of strawberries?

Ⓐ

Ⓑ

Ⓒ

Ⓓ

....

2. Tom has 14 marbles.

Kara has 15 marbles.

Who has an even number of marbles?

_____

Explain how you know with words or a model.

3. Which equation shows 12 as the sum of two even numbers?

Ⓐ $2 \times 6 = 12$

Ⓑ $8 + 8 = 12$

Ⓒ $5 + 7 = 12$

Ⓓ $6 + 6 = 12$

4. Leo adds 4 and 4. Will the sum be an even number or an odd number? Explain how you know using words or a model.

Name _____

Common Core Standards Practice

2.OA.C.4 Use addition to find the total number of objects arranged in rectangular arrays with up to 5 rows and up to 5 columns; write an equation to express the total as a sum of equal addends.

1. Look at the apples.

Write an equation to show the number of apples.

_____ + _____ + _____ = _____

....

2. Look at the pears.

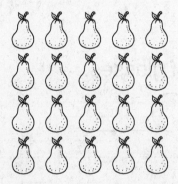

Write an equation to show the number of pears.

_____ + _____ + _____ + _____ = _____

3.

Write an equation to show the number of mugs.

___ ◯ ___ ◯ ___

4.

Write an equation to show the number of glasses.

___ ◯ ___ ◯ ___ ◯ ___ ◯ ___

5.

Write an equation to show the number of feathers.

___ ◯ ___ ◯ ___ ◯ ___ ◯ ___ ◯ ___

Common Core Standards Practice

2.NBT.A.1 Understand that the three digits of a three-digit number represent amounts of hundreds, tens, and ones; e.g., 706 equals 7 hundreds, 0 tens, and 6 ones. Understand the following as special cases: **a.** 100 can be thought of as a bundle of ten tens — called a "hundred." **b.** The numbers 100, 200, 300, 400, 500, 600, 700, 800, 900 refer to one, two, three, four, five, six, seven, eight, or nine hundreds (and 0 tens and 0 ones).

I. What is the value of the digit 3 in the number 392?

Ⓐ 3

Ⓑ 30

Ⓒ 300

Ⓓ 390

2. What is the value of the digit 7 in the number 117?

Ⓐ 1

Ⓑ 7

Ⓒ 70

Ⓓ 700

3. Complete the number sentence:

124 = _____ + 20 + 4

4. How many hundreds are there in 864? Explain how you know.

5. How many tens are in 182?

(A) 8

(B) 10

(C) 80

(D) 800

6. What is the value of the digit 6 in the number 604?

(A) 6

(B) 60

(C) 600

(D) 660

7. Complete the number sentence.

242 = 200 + _____ + 2

8. Look at the number 123.

a. What is the value of each digit in the number?

b. Write the number as a sum of the numbers in its three place values.

_____ ◯ _____ ◯ _____ ◯ _____

Name _____

Common Core Standards Practice

2.NBT.A.2 Count within 1000; skip-count by 5s, 10s, and 100s.

1. Count by 10s. Which number comes next?

60, 70, 80, 90, _____

Ⓐ 99

Ⓑ 100

Ⓒ 900

Ⓓ 990

2. Count by 100s. Which number comes next?

400, 500, 600, 700, _____

Ⓐ 100

Ⓑ 800

Ⓒ 900

Ⓓ 999

3. Count by 5s. What number comes next?

80, 85, 90, 95, _____

CC 11

4. Count by 100s. What number comes next?

200, 300, 400, 500, _____

5. Fill in the missing numbers.

880, 890, _____, 910, _____

6. Fill in the missing numbers.

450, _____, 650, 750, _____

7. What number comes next?

345, 350, 355, 360, _____

8. Jeremy skips-counts by 100 to 1000.
Which number does he NOT say?

(A) 300

(B) 700

(C) 910

(D) 1000

CC 12

Name _____

Common Core Standards Practice

2.NBT.A.3 Read and write numbers to 1000 using base-ten numerals, number names, and expanded form.

1. Which number is two hundred eighty-nine?

Ⓐ 892

Ⓑ 298

Ⓒ 289

Ⓓ 829

2. Which number is one hundred sixty-four?

Ⓐ 146

Ⓑ 614

Ⓒ 164

Ⓓ 416

Match the numerals with the names. Not all of the numbers have matches.

3. Two hundred fifty   202

4. Seven hundred sixteen   932

5. Nine hundred thirty-two   329

6. Two hundred two   760

7. Seven hundred sixty   525

8. Five hundred twenty-five   225

716

9. Which equals 516?

    Ⓐ 51 + 6

    Ⓑ 500 + 10 + 6

    Ⓒ 500 + 16 + 6

    Ⓓ 5 + 16

10. Which equals 228?

    Ⓐ 22 + 8

    Ⓑ 2 + 28

    Ⓒ 200 + 82

    Ⓓ 200 + 20 + 8

Complete each equation by writing the number in expanded form.

11. $347 = \underline{\hspace{2cm}} + 40 + 7$

12. $166 = \underline{\hspace{1.5cm}} + \underline{\hspace{1.5cm}} + \underline{\hspace{1.5cm}}$

13. $801 = \underline{\hspace{1.5cm}} + \underline{\hspace{1.5cm}} + \underline{\hspace{1.5cm}}$

14. $450 = \underline{\hspace{1.5cm}} + \underline{\hspace{1.5cm}} + \underline{\hspace{1.5cm}}$

15. $279 = \underline{\hspace{1.5cm}} + \underline{\hspace{1.5cm}} + \underline{\hspace{1.5cm}}$

16. $912 = \underline{\hspace{1.5cm}} + \underline{\hspace{1.5cm}} + \underline{\hspace{1.5cm}}$

Name _____

Common Core Standards Practice

2.NBT.A.4 Compare two three-digit numbers based on meanings of the hundreds, tens, and ones digits, using >, =, and < symbols to record the results of comparisons.

1. Which symbol goes in the circle to make the inequality true?

131 ◯ 129

Ⓐ >

Ⓑ =

Ⓒ <

Ⓓ +

2. Which symbol goes in the circle to make the inequality true?

448 ◯ 484

Ⓐ >

Ⓑ =

Ⓒ <

Ⓓ ×

Complete each inequality. Tell with words or a model how you know which number is greater.

3. 356 ◯ 401

4. 512 ◯ 509

5. Which statement compares 923 and 899?

    Ⓐ 923 > 899

    Ⓑ 923 < 899

    Ⓒ 923 = 899

    Ⓓ 923 + 899

6. Which statement compares 167 and 170?

    Ⓐ 170 > 167

    Ⓑ 170 < 167

    Ⓒ 170 = 167

    Ⓓ 170 × 167

Complete each inequality. Tell with words or a model how you know which number is less.

7. 772 ◯ 687

8. 513 ◯ 531

Name _____

Common Core Standards Practice

2.NBT.B.5 Fluently add and subtract within 100 using strategies based on place value, properties of operations, and/or the relationship between addition and subtraction.

Solve.

1. 16
   + 33

2. 89
   − 63

3. 32
   − 13

4. 46
   + 38

5. 48
   + 43

6. 56
   − 47

7. $82 - 28 =$ ☐

8. $73 + 18 =$ ☐

9. $28 + 74 =$ ☐

10. $41 - 36 =$ ☐

11. $96 - 44 =$ ☐

12. $67 + 76 =$ ☐

CC 18

Name _____

Common Core Standards Practice

2.NBT.B.6 Add up to four two-digit numbers using strategies based on place value and properties of operations.

1. Dana has 12 apples.
   She also has 14 mangoes and 16 oranges.
   How many pieces of fruit does she have in all?

   (A) 25   (B) 30   (C) 42   (D) 50

2. Aisha will find the sum of these numbers.

   $20 + 22 + 10 + 14 = \boxed{}$

   Which two numbers would you add first?
   Tell why.

   What is the sum?

   _____

3. Paul finds the sum of these numbers.

   $30 + 21 + 11 = \boxed{}$

   He adds 30 + 20 + 10, then adds 2. Is his sum
   correct? Tell how you know.

CC 19

4. Monica collects stickers.
She has 30 cat stickers, 30 butterfly stickers,
and 12 flower stickers.
How many stickers does she have in all?

Ⓐ 60

Ⓑ 75

Ⓒ 80

Ⓓ 72

5. Tell how you can find the sum of these
numbers. You can use words or models.

$15 + 18 + 20 + 25 = \boxed{}$

What is the sum?

_____

6. Find the sum:

$23 + 18 + 17 = \boxed{}$

_____

CC 20

Copyright © Pearson Education, Inc., or its affiliates. All Rights Reserved. 2

Name _____

Common Core Standards Practice

2.NBT.B.7 Add and subtract within 1000, using concrete models or drawings and strategies based on place value, properties of operations, and/or the relationship between addition and subtraction; relate the strategy to a written method. Understand that in adding or subtracting three digit numbers, one adds or subtracts hundreds and hundreds, tens and tens, ones and ones; and sometimes it is necessary to compose or decompose tens or hundreds.

1. Elise has 721 gold coins and 236 silver coins. How many coins does she have in all?

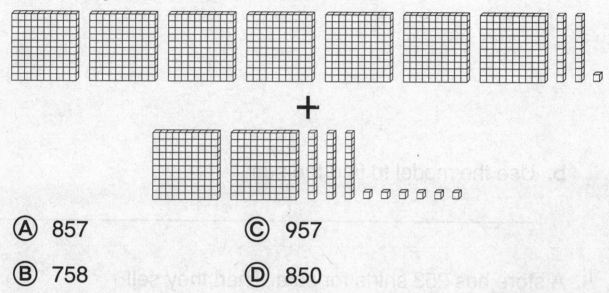

Ⓐ 857

Ⓒ 957

Ⓑ 758

Ⓓ 850

2. There are 356 people at a show. Then 171 people leave. How many people are left?
You can use the model to find the difference.

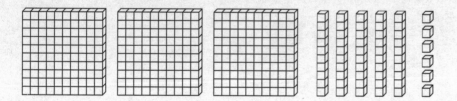

_____

3. Jason's father builds a wall with 542 bricks.
Jason adds 289 bricks.
How many bricks do they use in all?

   a. Draw a model to show the sum.

   b. Use the model to find the sum.

_____

4. A store has 253 shirts for sale. Then they sell
190 shirts. How many shirts remain?

   a. Draw a model to show the difference.

   b. Use the model to find the difference.

_____

Name _____

Common Core Standards Practice

2.NBT.B.8 Mentally add 10 or 100 to a given number 100–900, and mentally subtract 10 or 100 from a given number 100–900.

Find these sums or differences.

1. 290 − 10 = ☐

   Ⓐ 300

   Ⓑ 250

   Ⓒ 280

   Ⓓ 260

2. 390 + 10 = ☐

   Ⓐ 300

   Ⓑ 400

   Ⓒ 380

   Ⓓ 410

3.

470 + 10 = ☐ _____

4.

970 − 10 = ☐ _____

5.

800 − 10 = ☐ _____

Find these sums or differences.

6. $690 - 100 = \boxed{}$

    Ⓐ 590

    Ⓑ 680

    Ⓒ 700

    Ⓓ 600

7. $430 + 100 = \boxed{}$

    Ⓐ 330

    Ⓑ 440

    Ⓒ 530

    Ⓓ 500

8.

$470 + 100 = \boxed{}$ _____

9.

$770 - 100 = \boxed{}$ _____

10.

$180 - 100 = \boxed{}$ _____

Name _____

Common Core Standards Practice

2.NBT.B.9 Explain why addition and subtraction strategies work, using place value and the properties of operations.

1. Jeff adds these two numbers.

$$\begin{array}{r} 349 \\ +22 \\ \hline \end{array}$$

a. Can he add 3 and 2? Tell why.

_____

b. What is the sum? _____

. . . .

2. Tell two different ways to find the sum.
You can use words or models.

$$\begin{array}{r} 253 \\ +706 \\ \hline \end{array}$$

One way:

Another way:

3. Juan subtracts these two numbers.

357
− 194

a. What must he do to subtract the numbers in the tens place?

_____

_____

b. What is the difference? _____

4. Tell two different ways to find the difference.

414
− 178

One way:

_____

_____

Another way:

_____

_____

c. What is the difference? _____

Name _____

Common Core Standards Practice

2.MD.A.1 Measure the length of an object by selecting and using appropriate tools such as rulers, yardsticks, meter sticks, and measuring tapes.

1. Ahmed will measure the length of his book in inches. Which tool should he use? Tell why he should use that tool.

2. How long in inches is this crayon? Use an inch ruler to measure the length.

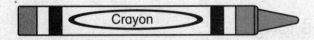

The crayon is _____ long.

3. Roger's father will measure the length of the family car. What tool should he use? Tell why.

4. How long is the rope? Use an inch ruler
to measure its width length.

The rope is _____ inches long.

5. Jeannie's mother needs to measure the width
of the windows in the living room. What tool
should she use to measure the width? Tell why.

6. How long is this figure?
Measure the figure in inches.

The figure is _____ inches long.

Name _____

Common Core Standards Practice

2.MD.A.2 Measure the length of an object twice, using length units of different lengths for the two measurements; describe how the two measurements relate to the size of the unit chosen.

1. Use a centimeter straight edge or meter stick to make these measurements.

 a. How wide is one window in the classroom? Measure in centimeters. Then measure in meters.

 The window is _____ centimeters wide.

 The window is _____ meters wide.

 b. Which measurement is greater?

 c. Which unit is larger?

2. Use an inch ruler or a yardstick to make these measurements.

 a. How wide is the classroom door? Measure in inches. Then measure in feet.

 The door is _____ inches wide.

 The door is _____ feet wide.

 b. Which measurement is greater?

 c. Which unit is larger?

The children in Mrs. Peters' class made measurements in their classroom. Circle the most likely unit for each measurement.

3. the width of the chalkboard

2 (centimeters, meters)

4. the length of a crayon

10 (centimeters, meters)

5. the height of the room

220 (centimeters, meters)

6. the length of a pencil

5 (inches, feet)

7. the height of a child

3 (inches, feet)

8. the width of a computer screen

15 (inches, feet)

Common Core Standards Practice

2.MD.A.3 Estimate lengths using units of inches, feet, centimeters, and meters.

Circle the best estimate for these lengths.

1. the height of a chair

3 inches   10 inches   25 inches

....

2. the length of a crayon

4 inches   12 inches   32 inches

....

3. the width of a child's desk

2 inches   20 inches   200 inches

....

4. the length of a school bus

2 feet   38 feet   380 feet

....

5. the height of a house with 2 floors

3 feet   10 feet   30 feet

Circle the best estimate for these lengths.

6. the width of a chair

4 centimeters   40 centimeters   400 centimeters

---

7. the width of a bracelet

1 centimeter   7 centimeters   30 centimeters

---

8. the height of a bottle of juice

14 centimeters   60 centimeters   100 centimeters

---

9. the height of an adult

2 meters   10 meters   20 meters

---

10. the length of a driveway to a house

2 meters   15 meters   600 meters

Name _____

Common Core Standards Practice

2.MD.A.4 Measure to determine how much longer one object is than another, expressing the length difference in terms of a standard length unit.

I. Use a centimeter ruler to measure these two pencils.

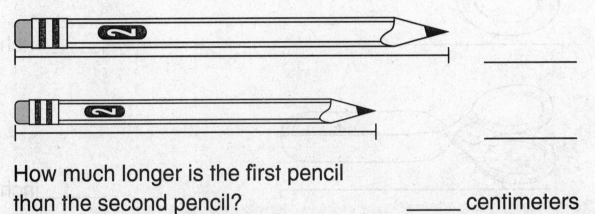

_____

_____

How much longer is the first pencil than the second pencil?   _____ centimeters

- -

2. Use an inch ruler to measure the crayon and the rope.

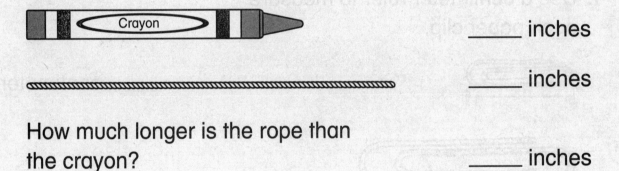

_____ inches

_____ inches

How much longer is the rope than the crayon?   _____ inches

3. Use an inch ruler to measure each scissors.

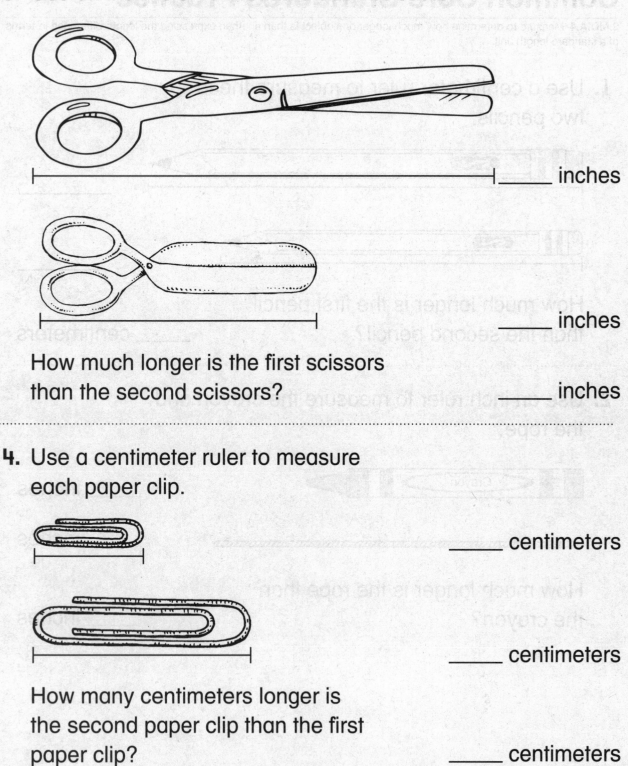

_____ inches

_____ inches

How much longer is the first scissors
than the second scissors?   _____ inches

....

4. Use a centimeter ruler to measure
each paper clip.

_____ centimeters

_____ centimeters

How many centimeters longer is
the second paper clip than the first
paper clip?   _____ centimeters

Name _____

Common Core Standards Practice

2.MD.B.5 Use addition and subtraction within 100 to solve word problems involving lengths that are given in the same units, e.g., by using drawings (such as drawings of rulers) and equations with a symbol for the unknown number to represent the problem.

1. Monica's table is 41 centimeters long.
Rebecca's table is 12 centimeters shorter
than Monica's.
How long is Rebecca's table?

Ⓐ 27 centimeters

Ⓑ 29 centimeters

Ⓒ 36 centimeters

Ⓓ 39 centimeters

2. Ellie has two pieces of ribbon. One piece is
27 inches. The other piece is 15 inches.

a. Draw a model to match the problem.

b. How many inches of ribbon does Ellie have?

_____

3. Jacob walks 65 meters from his classroom to the library. Then he walks 25 meters to the gym. How far does he walk?

Use the number line to show how far Jacobs walks.

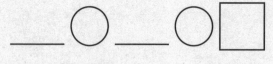

Write an equation to match the problem.

_____ ◯ _____ ◯ _____

How far does Jacob walk?

_____

4. A hot air balloon is 93 feet above the ground. Then it drops 75 feet. How far above the ground is it now?

Write an equation to match the problem.

_____ ◯ _____ ◯ ☐

Use ☐ for the unknown.

How high above the ground is the balloon?

_____

Name _____

Common Core Standards Practice

2.MD.B.6 Represent whole numbers as lengths from 0 on a number line diagram with equally spaced points corresponding to the numbers 0, 1, 2, ..., and represent whole-number sums and differences within 100 on a number line diagram.

I. Pencil A is 3 inches long.

Pencil B is 5 inches long.

Pencil C is 8 inches long.

Write A, B, and C on the number line to show each length.

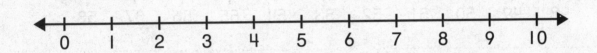

2. Use the number line below to represent this addition number sentence.

$45 + 6 =$ ☐

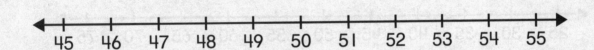

Use the number line to represent these number sentences.

3. $42 - 6$

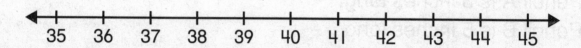

4. $58 - 9$

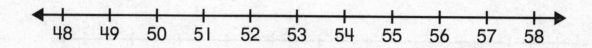

5. $81 - 7$

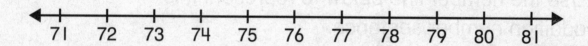

6. $25 + 25$

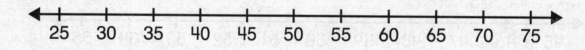

7. $70 - 15$

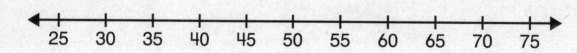

8. $85 - 30$

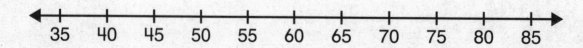

CC 38

Name _____

Common Core Standards Practice

2.MD.C.7 Tell and write time from analog and digital clocks to the nearest five minutes, using a.m. and p.m.

1. The clock shows the time that Joel's father wakes up every morning.

What time does Joel's father wake up?

Use A.M. or P.M.

_____ : _____

2. Sadie gets home from school every afternoon at the time shown on the clock below.

What time does Sadie get home from school?

Use A.M. or P.M.

_____ : _____

3. Math class begins after lunch.
The clock shows the time.

What time does math class begin?
Use A.M. or P.M.

_____ : _____

....

4. Mr. Jenkins comes home late one evening.
The clock shows the time.

What time does Mr. Jenkins come home?
Use A.M. or P.M.

_____ : _____

Name _____

Common Core Standards Practice

2.MD.C.8 Solve word problems involving dollar bills, quarters, dimes, nickels, and pennies, using $ and ¢ symbols appropriately. Example: If you have 2 dimes and 3 pennies, how many cents do you have?

1. Becky has the coins shown.
How much money does she have?

_____ ¢

···

2. Rosaline has three $1 bills, 1 quarter,
and 3 dimes.
How much money does she have?

_____

3. Jill has 87 ¢. Which set of coins could she have?

Ⓐ

Ⓑ

Ⓒ

Ⓓ

....

4. Abe has two $1 bills, 3 quarters, and 1 nickel. How much money does Abe have in all?

_____

Common Core Standards Practice

2.MD.D.9 Generate measurement data by measuring lengths of several objects to the nearest whole unit, or by making repeated measurements of the same object. Show the measurements by making a line plot, where the horizontal scale is marked off in whole-number units.

1. Measure with an inch ruler 5 pencils.
   Write the length of each pencil in the table.

Pencil	Length (inches)
1	
2	
3	
4	
5	

2. Put each measurement on the line plot.

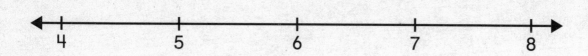

```
4        5        6        7        8
```

3. Measure with a centimeter ruler 5 books.
Write the length of each book in the table.

Book	Length (centimeters)
1	
2	
3	
4	
5	

4. Put each measurement on the line plot.

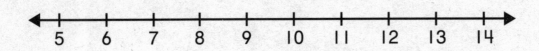

Name _____

Common Core Standards Practice

2.MD.D.10 Draw a picture graph and a bar graph (with single-unit scale) to represent a data set with up to four categories. Solve simple put-together, take-apart, and compare problems using information presented in a bar graph.

The table shows the number of books four students read this week.

Club Member	Number of Books
Judy	5
Eric	3
LaToya	2
Juan	4

1. Make a picture graph to show the data in the table.

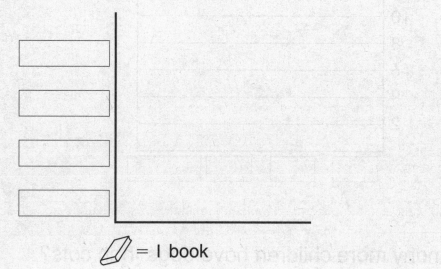

2. How many books did the four students read this week?

_____

The table shows the pets that the children in one class have.

Pet	Number of children
Bird	5
Cat	7
Dog	12
Hamster	3

3. Fill in the bar graph to match the data in the table.

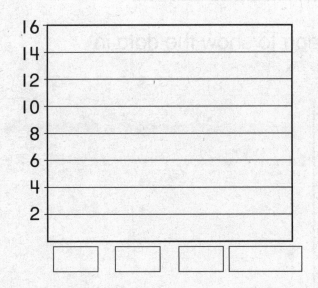

4. How many more children have dogs than cats? Tell how you know.

_____

Name _____

Common Core Standards Practice

2.G.A.1 Recognize and draw shapes having specified attributes, such as a given number of angles or a given number of equal faces. Identify triangles, quadrilaterals, pentagons, hexagons, and cubes.

1. Write the letter *Q* inside each shape that is a quadrilateral.

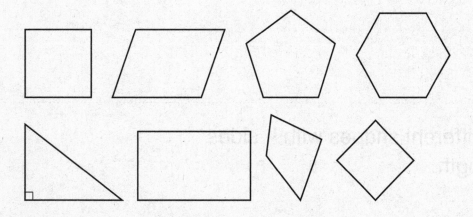

....

2. Name these shapes.

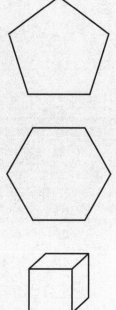

_____

_____

_____

3. Draw a shape with 3 sides of equal length.

....

4. Draw two different shapes with 4 sides
of equal length.

....

5. Draw a shape with 5 angles.

Common Core Standards Practice

2.G.A.2 Partition a rectangle into rows and columns of same-size squares and count to find the total number of them.

1.

a. Draw a line across the rectangle to make two smaller rectangles, each of the same size.

b. Draw two lines to divide the rectangles into equal-sized squares.

c. How many squares did you make? _____

- -

2. Divide the rectangle into 8 squares.

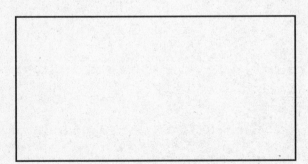

3.

[rectangle]

a. Draw two lines across the rectangle to make three smaller rectangles, each of the same size.

b. Draw three lines to divide the rectangles into squares.

c. How many squares did you make? _____

....

4. Divide the rectangle into 15 squares.

[rectangle]

Name _____

Common Core Standards Practice

2.G.A.3 Partition circles and rectangles into two, three, or four equal shares, describe the shares using the words halves, thirds, half of, a third of, etc., and describe the whole as two halves, three thirds, four fourths. Recognize that equal shares of identical wholes need not have the same shape.

I.

   a. Draw lines to divide the circle into
       4 equal parts. Shade one of the parts.

   b. What part of the circle is shaded? _____

   c. Circle the words that describe the whole circle.

       one fourth   two thirds   three fourths   four fourths

- -

2.

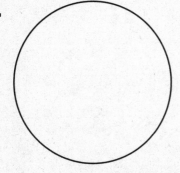

   a. Draw lines to divide the circle into 3 equal parts.
       Shade one of the parts.

   b. What part of the circle is shaded? _____

   c. Circle the words that describe the whole circle.

       one third   one half   two thirds   three thirds

CC 51

3.

a. Draw a line to divide the rectangle into 2 equal parts. Shade one of the parts.

b. What part of the rectangle is shaded? _____

c. Circle the words that describe the whole rectangle.

one half　　two halves　　two thirds　　three fourths

....

4. a. Divide the rectangle into 3 equal parts. What shape is each part? _____

b. Show another way to divide the rectangle into 3 equal parts. What shape is each part? _____

Name _____

Practice End-of-Year Assessment

1. Henry has two pieces of cloth. One piece is 12 inches long. The other is 25 inches long. How many inches of cloth does Henry have if he puts the two pieces together?

2. About how wide is the board in your classroom?

3. What is the value of the digit 2 in the number 324?

4. Find the sum of these numbers.

$$12 + 20 + 14 + 16 = \boxed{}$$

---

5. How many hundreds are in 724?

(A) 2

(B) 4

(C) 7

(D) 24

---

6. Jacob wants to measure the length
of his shoe.
What tool can he use?

7. Emily has 85 sheets of construction paper. She uses 34 sheets for a project. How many sheets of paper does Emily have left?

____ ◯ ____ ◯ ____

8. Draw a model to show 456 minus 173. Then find the difference.

_____

9. Andrew has a piece of string that is 82 inches long. Then he cuts 15 inches off the end of the string. How long is Andrew's string now?

10. Morrie measures the stem of a flower. It is 12 inches long. Aisha also measures the stem of the same flower. She finds it is 1 foot long.

    a. Why do Morrie and Aisha have different heights for the same stem?

    b. In a measurement of height, is the number of inches less than, equal to, or greater than the number of feet? How do you know?

11. Solve.

$$\begin{array}{r} 34 \\ -19 \\ \hline \end{array}$$

12. Andrew has the coins shown below.

How much money, in cents, does he have in all?

· ·

13. Julia read 510 pages. Jack read 479 pages.

Who read more pages? Tell how you know. Use a model or a number sentence to show.

14. A teacher arranges desks into 4 rows of 3.

Draw a model to match the desks.

How many desks are there?

- -

15. Find the sum.

$32 + 47 + 54 = \boxed{}$

- -

16. Mark has 42 marbles in one pile. He has 16 marbles in another pile. Draw a model to show the total number of marbles, and find the total.

17. Lucy's ribbon is 24 centimeters long.
Sarah's ribbon is 18 centimeters long.
How much longer is Lucy's ribbon?

18. Write the number 751 in expanded form.

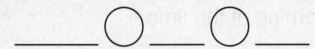

19. Clare made a block tower 32 inches tall.
Eric made a block tower 23 inches tall.
How many inches taller is Clare's tower?

CC 59

20. Use the number line to show 23 − 6.

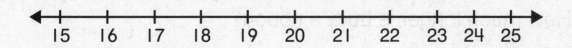

$$15 \quad 16 \quad 17 \quad 18 \quad 19 \quad 20 \quad 21 \quad 22 \quad 23 \quad 24 \quad 25$$

21. Solve.

$$94 - 78 = \boxed{}$$

22. Myron wakes up in the morning at the time shown on the clock.

What time does Myron wake up?
Include A.M. or P.M.

23. Divide the circle into 3 equal parts.

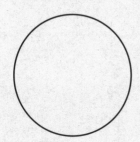

24. Use the number line to show the sum of 43 and 8.

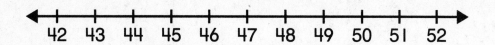

25. In a computer game, James scores
825 points. Erin scores 100 points more
than James. What is Erin's score?

26. Write the letter "P" inside the pentagon.

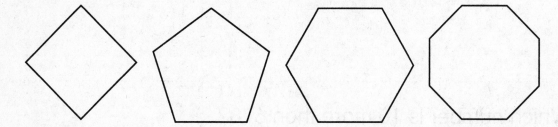

27.

a. Draw three lines across the rectangle to make four smaller rectangles, each the same size.

b. Draw four lines to divide the rectangles into squares.

c. How many squares did you make?

....

28. Which number is 10 more than 678?

(A) 688

(B) 668

(C) 778

(D) 578

29. Joy has 46 cents in her pocket.
She has 25 cents in her hand.
How many cents does Joy have in all?

....

30. Adam arranges oranges in the arrangement
shown below.

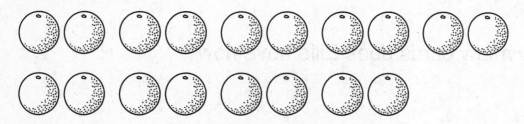

Does he have an even or odd number
of oranges? Tell how you know.

....

31. Find the next number in this sequence.

740, 750, 760, 770, _____

32. Ellie has 342 cards.
Sandra gives her 175 cards.

Draw a model to match the story problem.

How many cards does Ellie have now?

---

33. Draw a model to show this subtraction problem:
63 − 35

34. Which group does each figure belong? Write the letter of the figure in the correct box.

No equal parts	2 equal parts	4 equal parts

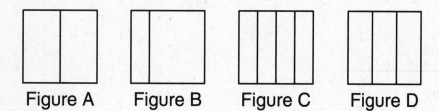

Figure A   Figure B   Figure C   Figure D

---

35. Emma divides the rectangle into 3 equal rows and 4 equal columns. How many squares are in the rectangle?

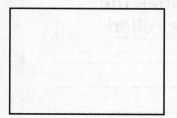

36. Pamela and her friends count the books that they read. The tally chart shows how many books they read.

Number of Books

Pamela	ЖII
Maria	ЖI
Diane	IIII

Complete the pictograph to match the tally chart.

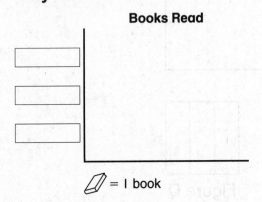

Books Read

= I book

---

37. Mia rolled a number cube 10 times. The table shows the results.

Number on cube	Number of times the number was rolled
I	I
2	2
3	2
4	0
5	3
6	2

Draw Xs to show Mia's results on a line plot.

I 2 3 4 5 6

38. Find the sum.

$12 + 85 = $ ☐

39. Complete each inequality. Tell with words or a model how you know which number is less.

349 _____ 352 | 531 _____ 513

40. Which of these is equal to 16? Circle Yes or No

$9 + 7$ Yes   No

$6 + 12$ Yes   No

$11 + 4$ Yes   No

$8 + 8$ Yes   No

Name _____

Performance Task I

Part A

Claire and her classmates are selling boxes of oranges. The table shows how many boxes of oranges they were sold in Weeks 1 and 2.

Boxes of Oranges Sold	
Week 1	27
Week 2	43

Claire wants to know how many boxes of oranges they sold in all.

I. How Claire can find the number of boxes of oranges they sold in week 1 and week 2. Show two ways to find the answer. Use pictures, numbers, or words.

Part B

One customer asks Claire how many oranges are in one box. Claire opens a box and this is what she sees.

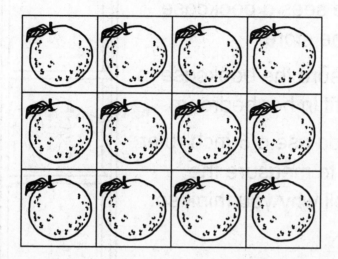

2. How can Claire find the number of oranges in a box?

3. How many oranges are in a box?

4. Is the number of oranges in a box an even or odd number? Tell how you know.

Name _____

Performance Task 2

Part A

Amanda will get a new bookcase for her bedroom. She sees a bookcase that she likes at the store.

Amanda will measure the bookcase to make sure it can fit in her bedroom.

1. Should Amanda use a 6-inch ruler or a yardstick to measure the bookcase? Tell why you think so.

Part B

The shelves in the bookcase are 16 inches high. Amanda wants to make sure her books will fit in the bookcase.

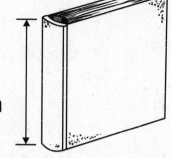

2. Find three different books in your classroom and measure their height.

Book 1: _____ Book 2: _____ Book 3: _____

3. Which books that you measured will fit in Amanda's bookcase?

Explain how you know which books will fit.